HISTOR

Eas[.]

LAURIE SIMMONS AND THOMAS H. SIMMONS

PHOTOGRAPHY BY
KATHLEEN ROACH

HISTORIC DENVER, INC.

To Liz and Julia, who took the journey with us.

This project was paid for in part by a State Historical Fund grant from the Colorado Historical Society with the assistance of Historic Denver, Inc.; Denver Community Planning and Development; Denver Office of Economic Development; Denver City Councilpersons Marcia Johnson, Doug Linkhart, Carol Boigon, and Jeanne Robb; Tattered Cover Book Store; Progressive Urban Management Associates; the American Institute of Architects Denver Chapter; Elizabeth Schlosser; and The Scientific and Cultural Facilities District.

Scientific & Cultural Facilities District

International Standard Book Number: 978-0-914248-01-9
Text, photographs and illustrations © 2007 Historic Denver, Inc. unless otherwise noted.

Cover photo: Savageau Building/Walgreen's Drugstore
photograph © 2007 Historic Denver, Inc.

All rights reserved. No portion of this book, either photographs or text, may be used or reproduced in any form without the written permission of the publisher except in the case of brief quotations embodied in critical articles and reviews.

Individually listed buildings are marked **N⊛R** for National Register of Historic Places and **D⊛L** for Denver Landmarks.

Published by Historic Denver, Inc.
1628 16th Street, Suite 200
Denver, Colorado 80202-1182

Printed by Mido Printing Company, Inc.

Editor: Lynne Hunt
Design and Composition: Cathy Calder, Blonde Ambition

Contents

Acknowledgments. 4
Introduction. 5
The Tour. 12
Selected Sources. 94
Selected Index. 95

This building at 3220-42 E. Colfax housed a number of retail stores and a restaurant serving residents and travelers. Its corner storefront is now home to the Goosetown Tavern (see Tour stop 38).

Acknowledgments

The authors offer sincere thanks to all those who assisted, supported, and encouraged this project. First and foremost, we acknowledge our debt to everyone who has worked to create, document, and preserve the history and architecture of East Colfax Avenue. Kathleen Brooker and Steve Turner of Historic Denver, Inc., envisioned the book and invited us to undertake the project. Kathleen Roach ably handled the photography. Lynne Hunt and Cathy Calder turned our words and pictures into a finished product. As always, Dale Heckendorn, National and State Register Coordinator for the Colorado Historical Society, selflessly shared information and expertise about businesses and architecture. Modupe Labode and Anne McCleave of the Colorado Historical Society reviewed the manuscript. Photographer and friend Roger Whitacre toured the avenue with us, offering recollections of more than sixty years in Denver and interviewing others with historic connections to the street. Colfax residents and business owners patiently answered our questions. Nancy Widmann generously provided us with copies of her work relating to the avenue. The incomparable staff of the Denver Public Library Western History and Genealogy Department, especially the unfailingly helpful Bruce Hanson, was indispensable. Liz Simmons assisted with historical research and editing and provided a 21st century perspective of the thoroughfare.

Portions of the historical background were developed as part of a Colorado Historical Fund survey and nomination grant project for East Colfax Avenue between Grant Street and Colorado Boulevard. The Colfax Business Improvement District sponsored and directed the project in 2006–07.

In the 1880s, large mansions graced East Colfax.
Shown here is the Charles M. Kittredge residence near Gaylord.
Denver Public Library, Western History/Genealogy Department

Introduction

The Beginnings: "Open Prairie"

Colfax Avenue first appeared on Denver maps in 1868, named for U.S. House Speaker Schuyler Colfax, who would later become Ulysses S. Grant's Vice President. Colfax visited the city in May 1865, and local boosters lobbied him to support Colorado's quest for statehood. To honor Colfax, the city dedicated the road along the southern boundary of central Denver to the Hoosier politician. Streets in the oldest portion of Denver were angled to comport with the channels of Cherry Creek and the South Platte River. Newer areas to the south and east followed east-west and north-south alignments and, as early Denver historian Jerome Smiley wrote, "the two great thoroughfares, Colfax Avenue and Broadway, were established as what may be called base-line streets for the eastern and southern new districts."

The area along Colfax Avenue east of Broadway developed slowly. By the end of 1879, *Rocky Mountain News* founder William N. Byers' residence at the northeast corner of Sherman and Colfax and a handful of other dwellings were present east of Broadway and north of Colfax; there were only two or three houses south of Colfax. Denverites considered the area to be out in the country and described it as "open prairie."

The Boom of the 1880s and the Growth of Rapid Transit

With the arrival of railroads in 1870, Denver's population surged from 4,759 to 35,629 in ten years. The 1880s saw a further doubling of population, with the city reaching 106,713 in 1890. Between Grant and Ogden streets, the western section of East Colfax emerged as an attractive residential area, while the street also served as the eastern entryway into downtown Denver. The thoroughfare was lined with large masonry mansions and had lawns bordered with trees. Residential development was sparser between Ogden and Gilpin streets, and between Gilpin and York streets the land was still vacant. No identifiable commercial buildings were present along the roadway.

Many subdivisions were platted along the 2.3-mile corridor between Grant Street and Colorado Boulevard. Private developers dictated lot sizes, block dimensions, and street alignments on the individual plats of the additions. Even Colfax Avenue itself took a slight northward jog

STREETCAR SERVICE MADE EAST COLFAX AN ATTRACTIVE LOCATION FOR BUSINESSES, THEATERS, AND APARTMENTS. HERE, A STREETCAR APPROACHES MARION.
DENVER PUBLIC LIBRARY, WESTERN HISTORY/GENEALOGY DEPARTMENT

between York and Josephine streets and followed a more northerly alignment east of that point.

Smiley observed that by 1887, "the city's expansion along Broadway and Colfax Avenue had begun, and the people and property owners along and adjacent to those streets were anxious for better transportation facilities than horse-car lines could afford, and were urging the building of cable roads." Developers agreed that improved transportation access to downtown would make their subdivisions more attractive to prospective homeowners. In 1886, a cable railway (whereby cars were powered by a cable laid in the street between the rails) extended to the western end of the corridor, linking the intersection of Grant and Colfax with downtown. When the system was abandoned after a year, property owners along East Colfax and Broadway offered the Tramway Company a cash bonus of approximately $200,000 to revive the cable cars and extend the lines out East Colfax to the vicinity of City Park and down Broadway to Alameda Avenue. The Tramway Company accepted the challenge and by December 1888, double tracks had been opened on Colfax past York Street with a loop to City Park.

The beginning of construction on the State Capitol building in 1886 also had a positive impact on the development of the corridor. The Capitol was erected on the tract bounded by East Colfax Avenue, Grant Street, East 14th Avenue, and Lincoln Street. The legislature did not meet in the building until 1895, and the Capitol was not formally completed until 1908.

Over the next few years the cable car tracks were extended further east along Colfax Avenue. In 1890, the Colfax Avenue Railway Company built a line from the terminus at York Street to Montclair. The company reorganized as the Colfax Electric Railway Company and extended its system to Fletcher (today's Aurora) in 1898. In 1899, the enterprise became part of Denver Tramway, which had replaced its cable cars with streetcars in 1893. This move facilitated transportation access, since streetcars ran faster than cable cars and could carry more passengers. The presence of the rapid transit line encouraged development at some distance from the city center. In the early 1890s, the National Jewish Hospital for Consumptives constructed a building at East Colfax and Jackson Street.

The Rise of Apartments and Building Diversification

The Panic of 1893 sent Denver and Colorado into an economic depression. Some large houses along the corridor were converted to multi-family units during this period. As the economy began to revive, developers built apartments along East Colfax, much to the alarm of residents of the surrounding neighborhood. Many residents believed such "tenements," "flats," or "terraces" would lessen the quality and property values of their neighborhood by being breeding grounds for disease and constituting a hazard to health and safety through perceived poorer construction practices than those employed for single family homes. In addition, residents feared that the higher population densities created by such buildings would erode their privacy.

In his 1901 history of the city, Jerome C. Smiley recognized the thoroughfare as one of the city's principal roadways, "Colfax being the great east-west avenue clear across its general geographical center." Continuous development (mostly residential in nature) along the street and north and south into adjacent neighborhoods extended as far east as Steele Street; a small area of vacant land remained between there and National Jewish Hospital to the east. Some commercial land uses also began to appear. The most intense early business development along the avenue was located near the intersection of East Colfax and York Street. A commercial nucleus of one-story storefronts was situated on both sides of the street on the blockfaces east of York. The Colfax Avenue Floral Company, with its large complex of greenhouses, operated to the east, on the north side of Colfax. The City Park Esplanade extended north from Colfax Avenue to City Park. The Detroit Apartments (1904) were located at the northeast corner of Colfax and Detroit, where a branch of the streetcar line turned north to provide access to the park. No other commercial or apartment buildings were located along Colfax between this point and Colorado Boulevard.

Increasing traffic along East Colfax Avenue led developers to push for the elimination of residential restrictions along the roadway. They pointed out that growing traffic diminished the avenue's desirability as a residential area and argued that Colfax was destined to evolve into a commercial corridor. Property owners in adjacent residential sections opposed removing the restrictions, but the corridor grew increasingly commercial.

After 1905, no new single family residences were built on East Colfax between Broadway and Garfield Street. In 1912, a coalition of booster and good roads groups joined forces in a drive to make East Colfax the best road in the state, seeking to turn the avenue into the gateway to Denver for tourists visiting by automobile from the East.

THE STATE CAPITOL AND THE CATHEDRAL OF THE IMMACULATE CONCEPTION ARE VISIBLE IN THE DISTANCE OF THIS CIRCA 1935 VIEW WEST FROM DOWNING STREET.
DENVER PUBLIC LIBRARY, WESTERN HISTORY/GENEALOGY DEPARTMENT

Automobiles and Construction in the 1920s

The automobile played a significant role in the development of East Colfax Avenue. The number of cars on the roads of Denver and the nation grew exponentially from the mid-1910s through the 1920s. East Colfax was paved prior to 1920, and in the mid-1920s, the street was designated as part of U.S. 40, a transcontinental highway extending from Atlantic City, New Jersey, to San Francisco, California.

In 1925, the City and County of Denver adopted a zoning code for the city. With a few exceptions, the faceblocks of East Colfax Avenue from Broadway to Yosemite Street were designated business or commercial. The city's first Master Plan document in 1929 described East Colfax as "formerly a principal residential street, and now in large part zoned for business and the principal artery through the Capitol Hill apartment district." A series of widenings along the avenue removed trees and terraced front lawns.

The 1920s saw a boom in commercial building construction along East Colfax. This expansion was driven by the street's status as a transcontinental highway, good streetcar access, and business zoning. A variety of commercial structures were erected along the avenue during the period: one-story buildings with multiple storefronts; multi-story buildings with storefronts on the first story and apartments above; and multi-story buildings with offices and storefronts. Significant educational, religious, entertainment, and special purpose facilities were also completed. Although construction declined precipitously during the Great Depression and World War II, a few commercial buildings and apartments were erected.

The Early Post World War II Years

During the period after World War II, automobile-oriented facilities proliferated along East Colfax, particularly in the eastern section adjacent to Aurora. Sprawling motels in U-shapes, L-shapes, or other configurations were erected. Restaurants incorporated eye-catching rooflines and unusual architecture to lure passing motorists. Signage was also an important element in roadside promotion and employed neon, flashing lights to give the illusion of movement, and symbols (Western themes, crowns, and arrows) to draw attention.

Locally owned and operated businesses still predominated along the avenue in the days before fast food chains. Drug store lunch counters and soda fountains along East Colfax were the place to go for a quick meal. The early postwar era saw a need for expanded business space to meet the demands of the area's growing population. Many older dwellings received commercial additions facing the avenue to house assorted retail and service firms.

East Colfax Avenue's transportation role continued to evolve. Streetcars ended their run on the avenue in 1950 and were replaced with buses. During 1964–68, completion of Interstate 70 to the north permitted transcontinental traffic to bypass the avenue, avoiding congestion and saving travel time. This change had a particularly negative impact on tourist-oriented accommodations on the street. As late as January 1968, a *Rocky Mountain News* columnist called Colfax Avenue "one of the most important gateways—east and west—to our town," carrying tourist and ski traffic as well as local east-west traffic. Despite the loss of traffic to Interstate 70, some new auto-oriented construction continued on East Colfax.

Transformations in the Late 20th Century

As a result of the Skyline Urban Renewal Project in downtown Denver in the late 1960s, new businesses moved to East Colfax Avenue. A 1993 *Denver Post* article explained: "The 1960s and 1970s also were the heyday of topless bars and sexually explicit theaters. Colfax became home to many of them. Denver razed blocks of seedy shops on Larimer Street in 1967 and some of them were reborn on Colfax." *Playboy* magazine labeled Colfax "the longest, wickedest street in America." Prostitution, drug dealing, and violence occurred along the thoroughfare. Conservative columnist George Will summarized the avenue's nadir in 1978: "The fear that [nuclear] war may blow civilization to smithereens loses some of its sting when you see Denver's Colfax Avenue."

East Colfax remained a major traffic arterial within the Denver metropolitan region. Chain store operations sited outlets along the avenue, typically featuring buildings set back from the street, with expanses of convenient parking and signage to entice passing motorists. The corridor featured numerous fast food chains (such as McDonald's, Burger King, and Starbucks), as well as non-food chains such as Blockbuster, Walgreen's, 7-Eleven convenience stores, and Conoco. The emergence of these franchises was associated with demolitions and redevelopment in some cases.

According to the Colfax Business Improvement District, $100 million was invested between 2000 and 2005 along East Colfax Avenue between Broadway and Colorado Boulevard, with an additional $100 million planned or under construction. Chamberlin Heights, at Steele Street, represented the first new residential development along Colfax in decades. In 2005, the Denver City Council approved Main Street zoning for the portion of East Colfax Avenue between Sherman and Albion streets. The action was the largest single rezoning in the city since the 1950s. The first Colfax Marathon took place in May 2006, with more than 6,000 persons participating in the twenty-six mile race from Aurora to Lakewood.

HISTORIC CURBSTONES BEARING THE STREET NAME STILL REMAIN AT LOCATIONS ALONG THE AVENUE.
PHOTO: THOMAS H. SIMMONS

THE TOUR

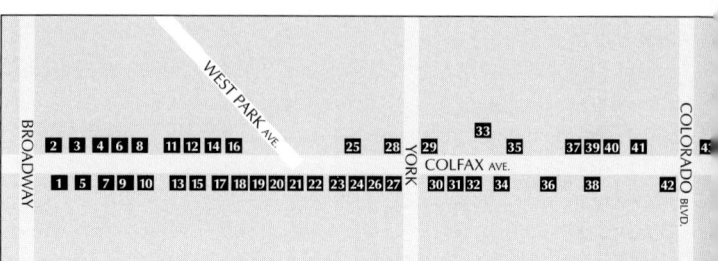

KEY

1. Colorado State Capitol
2. Colorado State Services Bldg.
3. Colorado State Office Bldg.
4. Argonaut Hotel
5. Newhouse Hotel
6. Silver State Savings and Loan Assoc. Bldg.
7. Cathedral Apartments
8. Cathedral of the Immaculate Conception
9. Utopia Flats
10. PenCol Apartment Bldg.
11. White Spot Restaurant
12. Mammoth Skating Rink/ Fillmore Auditorium
13. Royal Host Motel
14. Ogden Theater
15. Burtlock Apartments/ Smiley's Laundromat
16. West Vernon Hotel
17. The Colonnade
18. Seckler Dry Cleaning and Apartment Bldg./ Rosenstock Books
19. Altamaha Apartments/ Alta Court
20. Hamilton Apartments
21. Cooper House/Stanley Furs
22. Bohm-Griffith House/ Inglenook Apartments/ Holiday Chalet Hotel
23. Acobo Building
24. Kruse Restaurant/ Pete's Kitchen
25. The Leetonia
26. Weicker Transfer and Storage Company
27. Savageau Bldg./ Walgreen's Drugstore
28. Capitol Hill State Bank

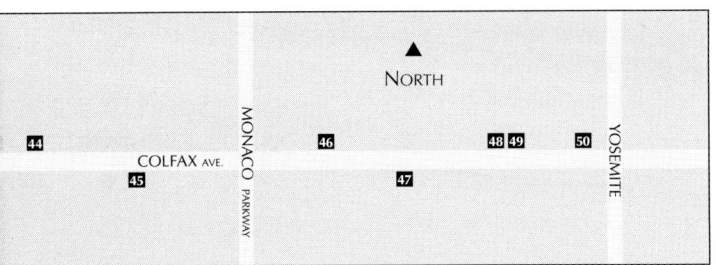

29 Park View Hotel/York View Apartments/Mierley Clinic/ Golden Apartments
30 Austin Building
31 Black and White Automotive Service/Maaco
32 Fifth Church of Christ, Scientist
33 East High School and City Park Esplanade
34 Bonfils Memorial Theater/ Henry Lowenstein Theater
35 The Detroit
36 Loustano House/Vogel Plumbing and Heating
37 Meyer's Kosher Meats
38 Hagans Jewelry/Block Floral
39 Intemann Candies/ Goodstein's Delicatessen
40 Thompson Theater/ Bluebird Theater
41 Bastien's Restaurant
42 National Jewish Hospital
43 Denver Orphans' Home/ Denver Children's Home
44 Weiss Drug Store
45 Eastmoor Beauty Shop
46 Miller's Groceteria/ Miller's Super Market
47 Chicken Delight
48 Westerner Motel
49 Sand and Sage Motor Court
50 Lazy-C Motor Lodge

1 COLORADO STATE CAPITOL
200 EAST COLFAX AVENUE

Architectural Style: CLASSICAL REVIVAL
Built: 1886–1908 Cost: $2,729,389
Architect: ELIJAH E. MYERS

Colorado's magnificent State Capitol is a fitting place to begin any tour of East Colfax Avenue, for it influenced the architecture and history of the thoroughfare and provided the avenue with its most imposing landmark. The Capitol had a less than auspicious beginning, as several years elapsed while state legislators delayed approving funds for construction. Henry C. Brown donated a ten-acre parcel for territorial government buildings in 1868. Brown's significance to early Denver history cannot be overestimated; he built the Brown Palace Hotel and established residential subdivisions on "Brown's Bluff," today's Capitol Hill. Although Colorado gained statehood in 1876, the land remained vacant, and Brown engaged in a long and ultimately unsuccessful legal bid to revoke his donation.

In 1881, Denver was selected as the state capital and the legislature passed acts for the building of a statehouse in 1883 and 1885. Detroit architect Elijah E. Myers, who designed four other state capitols, submitted drawings for a building with a Greek cross plan resembling that of the nation's Capitol. Myers promised his "Corinthian Order" building would be "the finest in the state." In 1889, the state abruptly dismissed Myers. Peter Gumry, James Murdoch, and Frank E. Edbrooke saw the building to completion in 1908.

The exterior walls of the massive building are composed of dark gray granite from the Zugelder Quarry in Gunnison County. Beulah red marble (Colorado rose onyx) and white Yule marble ornament the interior, along with stained glass, bronze finishings, and numerous works of art. Governor Davis H. Waite and executive officers occupied the partially finished building in 1894, and the first legislature met here the following year. Frank Edbrooke suggested that a golden dome would be appropriate for a gold producing state, so 24-carat gold leaf was applied in 1908.

THE CAPITOL'S FIRST STORY ROTUNDA CONTAINS MURALS BY DENVER ARTIST ALAN TRUE AND A POEM BY THOMAS HORNSBY FERRIL.

2 COLORADO STATE SERVICES BUILDING
1525 SHERMAN STREET
Architectural Style: FORMALIST
Built: 1957–1960 Cost: $3,756,000
Architects: GEORGE MEREDITH MUSICK, SR., AND TEMPLE H. BUELL

Completed in early 1960, this seven-story building became the first major structure erected by the state after the construction of the 1939 Capitol Annex at West 14th Avenue and Sherman Street. During World War II, government growth forced state agencies to find offices in downtown Denver buildings. This building was planned to consolidate the state's workforce. Departments such as Natural Resources, Agriculture, Institutions, and Public Welfare occupied the 180,000-square-foot building. The upper walls are clad with white Vermont marble, while Cold Springs, Minnesota gray granite adorns the base. A vertical emphasis is provided by the narrow, slightly inset windows.

3 COLORADO STATE OFFICE BUILDING
201 EAST COLFAX AVENUE
Architectural Style: CLASSICAL REVIVAL
Built: 1919–1921 Cost: $1,494,000
Architect: WILLIAM N. BOWMAN

Expanded responsibilities for state governments during World War I resulted in this building's construction on lots just north of the State Capitol in 1919–1921. Erected by Seerie and Varnum, the five-story building's walls are clad with gray Cotopaxi granite and are dominated by a series of fluted pilasters with composite capitals on the second through fourth stories. The interior contains a two-story lobby with a vaulted ceiling adorned with a stained glass skylight and a checkerboard floor composed of black and white marble squares. Two bronze mountain lion sculptures by Robert Garrison flank the Colfax Avenue entrance. A $4 million renovation in 1984–85 addressed safety issues and restored the building's original elegance.

The Colorado State Services Building, above, and the Colorado State Office Building, below, are both within the Civic Center Historic District.

The Colorado Department of Education occupies the Colorado State Office Building.

4 ARGONAUT HOTEL
233 EAST COLFAX AVENUE

Architectural Style: CLASSICAL REVIVAL
Built: 1912–1913 Cost: UNKNOWN
Architects: T. ROBERT WIEGER (1912); ROBERT WILLISON
AND MONTANA FALLIS (1913)

The Argonaut Hotel, which replaced a historic residence on this site, was built in two stages. In 1912, T. Robert Wieger designed the first three stories. Architects Robert Willison and Montana Fallis provided plans for two additional stories completed the following year. Wieger, who designed the Stanley Hotel in Estes Park, served in the U.S. Corps of Engineers during World War I and was chief engineer for the construction of General Hospital Number 21 (later Fitzsimons Army Hospital) in Aurora.

The hotel's brown brick walls are divided into bays by contrasting four-story buff brick pilasters and crowned by curvilinear parapets and finials above the elaborate bracketed cornice. White terra cotta enlivens the façade, framing the windows and composing other features. The U-shaped plan includes a front light court providing illumination and ventilation. Remodeling in 1960 clad the first story with aggregate panels of green stone.

George Snyder, Jr., a Denver real estate developer, was the original owner and builder of the 125-room hotel, once considered one of the city's most fashionable. Barbara E. Schwalbe, a widow, purchased the building in 1916, owning and managing it until her death twenty years later. Her son, O. Henry Schwalbe, succeeded her as the operator. The Colorado Hotel-Motel Association named Schwalbe its "Man of the Year" in 1963. The Argonaut's location across from the State Capitol grounds (see Tour stop 1) made it a favorite hangout of politicians. The Senate Lounge and the Quorum (a French restaurant run by Pierre Wolfe) opened in the building in 1960. The lounge attracted state and local lawmakers, while the restaurant won awards for its food, service, and atmosphere. The hotel shut its doors in 1973 and was remodeled as apartments for the elderly, becoming the Argonaut Hotel Apartments. The building is within the Civic Center Historic District.

The Argonaut Hotel occupies a prime location near the State Capitol that attracted many politicians before its conversion to apartments.

5 NEWHOUSE HOTEL
300 EAST COLFAX AVENUE

Architectural Style: COLONIAL REVIVAL/GEORGIAN
Built: 1911 Cost: UNKNOWN
Architect: ARTHUR H. O'BRIEN

Occupying a significant location across from the State Capitol is the Newhouse Hotel, a three-story red brick building with commercial enterprises on the first story. The building's corners and central bays feature banded brick quoins, and contrasting white terra cotta forms the window surrounds of the upper stories. The original cornice is missing; its place is marked by a band of white at the top of the walls. The building's central light court, visible on the west, is enclosed on the first story and serves as the hotel lobby. Murals of Colorado scenes painted by an unknown artist during the early 20th century are featured within.

This building replaced the large residence of Robert H. McMann, who moved to Denver from Ohio in 1875 and became a private banker, director of the Federal National Bank, and president of his own real estate and investment firm. After retiring from business, McMann moved to California, returning to Denver during the summers. The Cedar Investment Company, believed to be one of his ventures, took out a building permit for a brick hotel on this site in 1911.

The street level storefronts of the Newhouse, now altered from their original appearance, accommodated a variety of businesses that appealed to occupants of the hotel and residents of the Capitol Hill neighborhood. In 1924, the businesses included a millinery, a tailor shop, a laundry, an art company, and a barber. Capitol Hill Books has occupied the northwest corner for almost three decades.

Like many early 20th century hotels and apartments, the Newhouse boasted a light court, providing occupants with sunshine and fresh air.

6 SILVER STATE SAVINGS AND LOAN ASSOCIATION BUILDING
1500 GRANT STREET

Architectural Style: FORMALIST
Built: 1963–1964 Cost: $1,000,000
Architect: WILLIAM C. MUCHOW

Architect William C. Muchow reported that the design of this four-story precast concrete building took inspiration from the classical composition of the State Capitol, captured in magnificent views from its windows (see Tour stop 1). The 1959 Colorado State Services Building (see Tour stop 2), a block to the west, may also have been influential. The building's Formalist style was immensely popular for Denver's financial institutions from the late 1950s through the early 1970s. Predating this example were Raymond Harry Ervin's 1958 First National Bank and the 1962 Western Federal Savings on 17th Street. In 1968, Muchow worked on the iconic Federal Reserve Branch Bank, built on 16th Street in the Formalist style. Occupying a prominent geographic location, the Silver State building was designed to be viewed from all directions and has identical upper floors on all sides. The exterior features modernistic precast panels, although the inside is designed with as many natural finishes as possible, including travertine marble, dark walnut, and Virginia slate.

Otis Archie King, who made a fortune selling a mining claim to Climax Molybdenum Company, founded Silver State Savings and Loan in 1923. After World War II, Denver's population and its role as the financial center of the Rocky Mountain region expanded, and Silver State opened branches on Welton Street, in the Cherry Creek and Lakeside shopping centers, and in Aurora and Colorado Springs. In the 1960s, the company became a subsidiary of San Diego Imperial Corporation, then the largest savings and loan enterprise in the world. As the Colorado headquarters of Silver State, this building included drive-up windows and ample parking on the first story. Escalators and elevators ferried customers to the open bank lobby and service departments above. The fourth story, rented to other firms, was inset from the others and clad in glass, with an overhanging roof sheltering the walls below.

The Colorado Education Association, an organization dating to 1875, moved into this former savings and loan building in 1995.

7 CATHEDRAL APARTMENTS
400 EAST COLFAX AVENUE

Architectural Style: 20TH CENTURY COMMERCIAL/ART DECO
Built: 1923   Cost: $50,000   Architect: UNKNOWN

Following 20th century trends along East Colfax Avenue, this 1923 tan brick building with contrasting dark brown brick includes commercial storefronts facing the thoroughfare on the first story and apartments above. Originally planned as a one-story brick building with a basement, the design was modified and a second building permit was obtained to construct an additional story. Jackson Realty & Investment Company, owners of the land since 1906, erected the $50,000 building. The apartments are situated directly across from the 1912 Immaculate Conception Cathedral (see Tour stop 8), whose spires rise to the north, and from which it takes its name.

In many ways typical of 20th Century Commercial style buildings with multiple storefronts found throughout Colorado, the Cathedral Apartments is distinguished by its Art Deco detailing on the second story. A series of arched-top projections enframed by pilasters of bricks set at an angle rise above the flat roof and have stucco faces ornamented with sculptural terra cotta and protruding bricks. The L-shaped building featured one large commercial space extending through the full length of the wing at the west end and five stores on the remainder of the first story.

The Alta Market occupied the large space on the west after the building was completed. A later business in the storefront was the Marcove Drug Company, which continued in this location for more than two decades. Tenants in the smaller stores in 1924 included: Joseph Gangel's delicatessen, replaced in the 1930s by the Cathedral Food Shop Restaurant and later by Corfield Photography Studio; Mrs. Clara Stover's Candies, later known as Mrs. Stover's Bungalow Chocolates; the Junior League Shop, succeeded by Nelson Apparel Shop and Slack's Women's Wear; and the clothes cleaning business of Agnes M. De Vano, later known as Madame De Vano Dry Cleaners.

The Cathedral Apartments combines commercial and domestic functions and is distinguished by its Art Deco ornament.

8   CATHEDRAL OF THE IMMACULATE CONCEPTION
401 EAST COLFAX AVENUE

Architectural Style: FRENCH GOTHIC
Built: 1902–1912   Cost: $500,000
Architects: LEON COQUARD, AARON M. GOVE AND THOMAS F. WALSH

When plans for this building were conceived, Capitol Hill was Denver's elite neighborhood and its prominent Catholic residents devoted themselves to making the dream of a magnificent cathedral on this site a reality. Groundbreaking ceremonies for the new cathedral occurred in 1902, but a lack of funds delayed its completion for a decade. In October 1912, John Cardinal Farley of New York and Reverend Hugh L. McMenamin climbed scaffolding to bless the twin 210-foot spires as they dedicated the cathedral with a program attended by thousands.

The cruciform plan cathedral is constructed of gray Bedford, Indiana, limestone atop a foundation of Gunnison County granite. The $500,000 building is cited as Denver's finest example of the French Gothic style. Detroit architect Leon Coquard produced the original plans, and Aaron M. Gove and Thomas F. Walsh saw the project to completion. The cathedral's spires became instant visual landmarks along the avenue, rivaling the gold dome of the State Capitol for attention. The eastern spire houses fifteen bells. The interior features a sixty-eight-foot vaulted ceiling, altars and statuary of Carrara marble, seventy-five Bavarian stained glass windows, and spiral staircases leading to balconies providing views of the Rocky Mountains. A small landscaped area east of the building provides a rare spot of green along the avenue.

Designated a minor basilica in 1979, the cathedral received a $2.5 million restoration before Pope John Paul II's visit in 1993. The cathedral's mission has evolved along with the neighborhood. Today it is considered a haven along East Colfax Avenue, providing tens of thousands of meals to the poor and homeless each year, as well as three daily and six Sunday masses for the faithful each week.

As the Cathedral approached completion in 1912,
lightning struck the west tower, taking off the top twenty-five feet.
Photo: L.C. McClure, Denver Public Library, Western History/Genealogy Department

9 UTOPIA FLATS
420 EAST COLFAX AVENUE

Architectural Style: BEAUX ARTS
Built: 1902 Cost: $35,000
Architect: EUGENE R. RICE

Denver architect Eugene R. Rice designed the three-story Utopia Flats as a luxury apartment building. Built in 1902, the building reflected the growing acceptance of multi-family housing in the Capitol Hill neighborhood. During the 1890s, a few apartments were built in the area, igniting fears that their presence would change the upscale character of the neighborhood. Critics soon dubbed the area flanking East Colfax Avenue as "Flatburg," but developers found that apartment houses were excellent investments. Before World War I, the buildings were often given grand names like those of hotels. To reassure homeowners that apartments were not a threat, the city required such buildings to be constructed with substantial material and plenty of space, light, and ventilation.

Utopia Flats, erected and owned by contractors Alexander Brown and Conrad Schrepferman, featured twelve apartments through 1934. The following year, Luzerne A. Richey acquired the building and hired architect Walter H. Simon to design alterations that created retail spaces on the first story facing East Colfax Avenue and offices and apartments on the upper floors. Richey, a Denver attorney and real estate developer, had an office in the building and his son and daughter-in-law lived in one of the apartments. The 1935 remodeling created six commercial spaces which, by the 1940s, housed tenants such as the Nob Hill Inn, a restaurant that continues to operate here. Other businesses included Crown Jewelers, Cactus Shop Gifts, Pen Cove Beauty Salon, Kober's Book Shop, and Reese House No. 3 Restaurant. The jewelry store, beauty salon, and restaurant were all still in the building in the 1960s.

Utopia Flats' Beaux Arts design is reflected on the upper stories, corresponding to its original function as a luxury apartment building.

10 PENCOL APARTMENT BUILDING
504 EAST COLFAX AVENUE

Architectural Style: LATE 19TH AND EARLY 20TH CENTURY REVIVALS
Built: 1925   Cost: UNKNOWN
Architect: WALTER H. SIMON

Green clay tiles, red brick walls, and white terra cotta trim distinguish the PenCol Apartment Building designed by Walter H. Simon in 1925. The architect established his own firm in that year, and the commission was one of his first major projects. The name for the building is derived from its location at the prominent corner of East Colfax Avenue and Pennsylvania Street. Reflecting the evolution of the avenue, the building replaced a large 19th century residence that stood on the site. Contractor Henry Aronoff, a Russian immigrant, was the builder and co-owner of the PenCol. His partner was Milton Morris, a Denver lawyer and developer who financed several apartments in the city. Together the men were principals of the Aromor Investment Company, which participated in a large number of real estate transactions. Walter Simon also worked on the Aromor Apartment Hotel for the firm.

Like most apartment buildings erected on the avenue during the 1920s, the PenCol featured street level commercial spaces facing the thoroughfare. A continuous terra cotta storefront cornice divides the business floor from the luxury apartments above. They are accessed by an entrance on the west elaborated with a terra cotta frontispiece and sheltered by a metal canopy with decorative glass trim. The PenCol Drugstore operated in the northwest corner of the building for many years. Azriel Stein, a native of Pittsburgh and a pharmacist, owned and operated the business. Neighborhood residents obtained prescriptions, drank sodas and ate ice cream, and shopped for gifts at the drugstore. Other businesses in the building in the early years included a produce market, a restaurant, a florist, and a bakery operated by William Bender.

INSET WALL DORMERS OF THE
PENCOL APARTMENTS FEATURE
CURVILINEAR PARAPETS WITH FINIALS
AND WROUGHT IRON BALCONETS.

11 WHITE SPOT RESTAURANT
601 EAST COLFAX AVENUE

Architectural Style: GOOGIE
Built: 1967 Cost: UNKNOWN
Architect: ARMET AND DAVIS

An excellent example of the Googie style was added to East Colfax Avenue in 1967 in the form of a White Spot Restaurant. The building's unusual architecture is an expression of the style that originated with a California coffee shop of that name after World War II and became popular along highways and major thoroughfares throughout the country. The style was viewed as futuristic, displaying features such as cantilevered and tilting roofs, walls, and windows, as well as geometric shapes and acute angles. The style also used expanses of glass, metal, plastic panels, and stone veneers. The architects for this building, Armet and Davis of Los Angeles, are considered the preeminent designers in the Googie style.

The White Spot coffee shop chain started in Colorado in 1947. William F. Clements, who was born in Monte Vista, operated a bakery business that supplied restaurants in downtown Denver before opening his first White Spot in an existing storefront on Broadway. Clements created nine restaurants in the chain and hired Armet and Davis as the firm's architects. The coffee shops were known for their casual atmosphere, convenient parking, attractive prices, fast and friendly service, comfortable seating, and menus with a wide selection of meals. The avenue's White Spot operated until the mid-1980s, and the last representative of the chain closed in 2001. A series of restaurants followed in this building, but none achieved long-term success until Tom's Diner, owned by Thomas S. Messina, began serving food in 1999.

This Googie style restaurant has a dynamic roof consisting of four geometric plates radiating from a central structure containing utilities. A local artists' group painted the 1970s-themed mural on the roof.

12 MAMMOTH SKATING RINK/ FILLMORE AUDITORIUM
801 EAST COLFAX AVENUE/ 1510–1544 CLARKSON STREET

Architectural Style: 20TH CENTURY ECLECTIC
Built: 1907   Cost: $32,000
Architect: EDWIN H. MOORMAN

Architect Edwin H. Moorman provided this "mammoth" building with a design you might expect to see in an English resort town or an amusement park. The architecture reflects the building's original function as a roller skating rink. In 1907, the Mammoth Skating Rink Company, headed by Samuel Cohen, purchased a vacant tract of land and erected this $32,000 recreation facility. The building also included an "up-to-date" restaurant serving soft drinks. One newspaper noted, "Roller skating is all the rage over the country at present, and this will be the first high-class rink to be opened in Denver."

The skating craze faded and in 1911, the Fritchle Automobile and Battery Company leased the building for its car manufacturing operations. Oliver P. Fritchle started a battery repair shop in Denver in 1903, and two years later began manufacturing batteries and electric cars. Fritchle's output included about 2,000 cars in a variety of styles, including one automobile that could travel 100 miles without recharging. Production of the cars stopped in 1917, after the electric self-starter on competing gasoline vehicles was perfected.

In subsequent years the building saw use as an automobile storage and repair facility, an ice and roller skating rink, a place for sporting events, a multi-purpose recreation center, and a warehouse. In 1970, George Green of New Jersey turned it into a famous venue for rock concerts, hosting such performers as Jethro Tull, the Grateful Dead, and Joe Cocker. In 1987 it became the Mammoth Events Center, accommodating concerts, sporting events, and conventions. In 1991, the historic Clarkson Hotel to the south was demolished, and a new entrance plaza and ticketing area were created facing the avenue. Since 1999, the building has been known as the "Fillmore Auditorium," in tribute to the entertainment venue in San Francisco.

The former roller skating rink features soaring domed towers, red and buff brick, strapwork ornaments, and large arched windows.

13 ROYAL HOST MOTEL
930 EAST COLFAX AVENUE

Architectural Style: INTERNATIONAL STYLE
Built: 1966 Cost: UNKNOWN Architect: UNKNOWN

The Royal Host Motel is notable in Denver's filmography for having appeared in the 1978 motion picture *Every Which Way but Loose*, directed by James Fargo and starring Clint Eastwood and his orangutan companion, "Clyde." In one scene, Eastwood, playing a guest at the motel, rides in the exterior glass elevator to the street and walks east across the street to the still existing 7-Eleven.

This 1966 hostelry contrasts architecturally with the earlier hotels and tourist courts along East Colfax through its five-story, fifty-four-room modern composition featuring a projecting elevator tower at the northeast corner, balconies with metal panel balustrades topped by metal railings, a flat unadorned roof, stucco walls, and a fifth floor penthouse. The motel represents the International Style, a product of the German Bauhaus movement, reflected also in the rectangular form and the strong horizontal emphasis overlaid with vertical elements. Exterior doors to all units provided travelers with easy access to the associated parking lot, a nod to the importance of the automobile and the street's role as part of U.S. 40. The elaborate neon motel sign at the northeast corner of the property, a popular subject for photographs, features a crown—an image frequently found on motel advertising of the period.

THE ROYAL HOST IS AN EXAMPLE
OF THE INTERNATIONAL STYLE APPLIED
TO MOTEL DESIGN.

14   OGDEN THEATER
935 EAST COLFAX AVENUE

Architectural Style: MEDITERRANEAN REVIVAL
Built: 1917   Cost: UNKNOWN
Architect: HARRY W. J. EDBROOKE

Douglas Fairbanks starred in *Wild and Woolly*, the first film shown when the Ogden Theater opened in September 1917. The Ogden's owners, J. A. Goodridge and John Thompson, also operated an older theater (now known as the Bluebird, Tour stop 40) further east on the avenue. In 1927, the partners built a third theater in Capitol Hill, the Hiawatha (now the Esquire) on Downing Street. Goodridge, a veteran theater manager from Alamosa, and Thompson, a successful Denver grocer, were principals of the International Amusement Company (IAC). Harry W. J. Edbrooke, nephew of Denver pioneer architect Frank Edbrooke, created the two-story Mediterranean style design for the Ogden with identical corner towers, brick walls, red tile roofing, a bracketed cornice, polychromatic terra cotta, and a frieze with beautiful tiled panels. At the center of the frieze, two winged cherubs flank the IAC monogram.

The owners boasted the building was "absolutely the best appointed and most convenient of all theaters." Originally, the Ogden was a second-run theater, showing movies a week or two after they played at downtown venues. In addition to motion pictures, moviegoers saw newsreels four times and vaudeville acts three times each week. Because the theater expected to draw its customers from the immediate neighborhood and from those who used public transportation, there was no planned parking. During the 1920s, the building was improved with an expanded balcony, a marquee, a remodeled entrance, and a pipe organ. The theater remained under the same ownership and management until 1964. After a subsequent series of operators, the Landmark Theaters took over the Ogden in 1977, notably screening the *Rocky Horror Picture Show* at midnight on Saturdays for almost thirteen years. In 1990, concert promoter Doug Kauffman purchased the building and rehabilitated it as a concert hall.

The Ogden Theater is one of the few surviving representatives of the golden age of motion pictures in Denver.

15 BURTLOCK APARTMENTS/ SMILEY'S LAUNDROMAT
1062–1080 EAST COLFAX AVENUE

Architectural Style: ART DECO
Built: 1932 Cost: UNKNOWN Architect: UNKNOWN

This fine Depression era example of Art Deco style incorporates a number of remarkable architectural features, including a tiered cornice of alternating brick and tile; brick walls with streamlines and string courses; zigzag bays, including the angled corner bay on the northeast; and oriel windows on the northwest. The projecting metal storefront cornice, glazed black brick, and wide expanses of glass on the first story are equally noteworthy.

The building opened in 1932, with the Burtlock Apartments occupying the upper stories and five commercial ventures at street level. Original firms in the building were Marguerite Krier's beauty parlor, John Simeone's fruit market, the Herring and Hensman restaurant, and Herbert C. Martin's grocery. By the following year, a chain drugstore, Walgreen's, also located here. Another branch of Walgreen's already operated twelve blocks further east on the avenue (see Tour stop 27). The first beauty parlor was replaced by the Aristocrat Beauty Salon, operated by Ada Mann in the same location for decades. The restaurant became the Chicken Inn during the 1940s and Hersh's Coffee Shop during the 1950s. Walgreen's was replaced by the Sam Frank Drug Company, which was a longtime tenant.

In 1980, Art Cormier created Smiley's Laundromat, which occupied the entire first story and became one of the best-known businesses on the avenue. Cormier, a real estate entrepreneur, headed the Colorado Investment and Mortgage Company. He believed, "Colfax is Denver. There's more history on Colfax than Larimer ever had." Smiley's boasts that it is the world's largest laundromat, containing hundreds of washers and dryers. Despite its gargantuan size, it is known for being impeccably clean, cheap, and friendly. It serves as a meeting ground for a diverse clientele.

Known today as Smiley's Laundromat, this 1932 building is an excellent example of the Art Deco style in Denver.

16 WEST VERNON HOTEL
1201–1225 EAST COLFAX AVENUE

Architectural Style: MEDITERRANEAN REVIVAL
Built: 1905 Cost: UNKNOWN
Architect: EDWIN H. MOORMAN

Prominent Denver real estate developer John S. Flower erected the West Vernon Hotel in 1905. Flower's original plan called for a one-story retail building, a proposal which drew strong opposition from wealthy owners of surrounding single family homes who opposed the expansion of commercial land uses. The developer's alternative, a residential hotel, was apparently more palatable, although its first story contained six storefronts in addition to the hotel lobby. Edwin H. Moorman, who also designed the Mammoth Skating Rink (see Tour stop 12), was the architect for the building. The three-story hotel features an elaborated round arch entrance facing East Colfax surmounted by oriel windows on the upper stories. The building's stucco walls, wrought iron balconies with massive ornamented brackets, and occulus windows reflect its Mediterranean influences.

In addition to the hotel, long-time tenants in the building included the Speth Floral Company, the Wellworth Five, Ten and Twenty-Five Cent Store, and a branch of the Westminster Laundry. Sid King operated the Calvert Inn Restaurant and Bar here in the 1950s. Responding to the declining character of the avenue in the 1960s, he converted the establishment to the Crazy Horse Bar, a burlesque club whose dancers disrobed as King played emcee and commentator. Scenes from Clint Eastwood's *Every Which Way but Loose* (1978) were filmed at the Crazy Horse. Financial problems forced King to close in 1983. In 1985, the building underwent rehabilitation. It is now known as Bourbon Square and houses offices and retail establishments.

Reflecting the avenue's evolution, this building has housed a hotel, a burlesque club, and, following rehabilitation, offices.

17 THE COLONNADE
1210 EAST COLFAX AVENUE

Architectural Style: RENAISSANCE REVIVAL
Built: 1902   Cost: $100,000
Architect: CHARLES QUAYLE

Swedish immigrant John Holmberg changed the face of East Colfax Avenue during the early 20th century, erecting the $30,000 Corona Flats in 1900 (no longer standing), the Altamaha Apartments (one block east, see Tour stop 19), and this building in 1902. Both the Colonnade and the Altamaha addressed Denver's growing taste for luxury apartment buildings, which modeled itself after a similar trend that began in New York and seemed appropriate for sophisticated Capitol Hill. Luxury apartments incorporated such cutting edge features as central heat, elevators with attendants, rooftop gardens, and special rooms for social and other activities.

Holmberg's 1902 buildings are similar in their size and shape, but the tan brick and terra cotta Colonnade displays a more elaborate façade with an imposing central portico (now enclosed with glazing) of massive three-story fluted columns supporting an entablature with a terra cotta frieze ornamented with garlands and medallions. The projecting hipped roof wings have hipped roof dormers, stone quoins, and windows with varied terra cotta ornament. On the west wall toward the front, each story has an inset balcony. The interior of the $100,000 Colonnade boasts frosted and leaded European glass and fireplaces. Its cost was 40 percent more than the Altamaha down the street.

Charles Quayle came from a family of Denver architects who helped shape the early city. Among their works were more than twenty-five schools. Most of Charles Quayle's buildings produced during 1880–1907 have been demolished, making this example very significant. He is also credited with the Pitkin County Courthouse in Aspen. In 1907 he joined his brother, Edward, in San Diego, California, where the Quayles continued their careers. Charles Quayle died there in 1940.

The $100,000 Colonnade represented luxury apartment living in Denver in 1902.

18 SECKLER DRY CLEANING AND APARTMENT BUILDING/ ROSENSTOCK BOOKS
1228–1240 EAST COLFAX AVENUE

Architectural Style: EXOTIC REVIVAL
Built: 1924   Cost: $40,000   Architect: UNKNOWN

Development accelerated along the avenue during the 1920s, when each new business competed with those around it to attract the attention of passersby. In 1924, the Seckler Dry Cleaning Company completed this exotic three-story eye-catching building with a façade of white glazed brick and terra cotta with projecting parapets. Warren C. Seckler, a native of Ohio who came to Denver in 1906, financed this exquisitely decorative building to contain his dry cleaning business, other commercial firms on the street level, and apartments, including his own residence, above. It is possible that the construction incorporated parts of an earlier building on the site (see the arched windows with stone sills on the west wall).

Seckler Dry Cleaning occupied the western storefront (1228) through 1958 and also utilized a separate one-story building on the alley. Other businesses here during his tenure included a furrier, a clothing store, a grocer, and real estate firms. After Seckler's death, Fred Rosenstock brought his bookstore and publishing business into the building in 1962. Rosenstock came to the United States from Austria as a child, grew up in New York, and moved to Denver for his health after serving in World War I. In 1922, he opened the Denver Book Shop on Stout Street, operating it with his wife, Frances. Together they started the Bargain Book Store, a business that survived the Great Depression by making extensive sales of textbooks to schools. The couple developed a national reputation for their trade in Western Americana, supplying private collectors, universities, and the Denver Public Library. Fred Rosenstock's biographer, Donald E. Bower, judged that the bookseller helped make Denver "one of the major centers of reference materials on the old West." In 1975, Rosenstock disposed of his books and began dealing in Western art. He died in 1986, at the age of 102.

THE SECKLER BUILDING'S
UNIQUE BLEND OF WHITE GLAZED BRICK,
TERRA COTTA, AND EXOTIC DESIGN
INFLUENCES ATTRACTS ATTENTION
ALONG EAST COLFAX.

19. ALTAMAHA APARTMENTS/ALTA COURT
1300–1326 EAST COLFAX AVENUE/ 1490 LAFAYETTE STREET

Architectural Style: RENAISSANCE REVIVAL
Built: 1902 Cost: $59,000
Architect: GEORGE L. BETTCHER

The buff brick and white limestone Altamaha Apartments is another early 20th century representative of luxury apartment construction. Completed in 1902, the apartments facing the avenue are joined by a bracketed cornice to a smaller building on Lafayette Street. Swedish developer John Holmberg erected five apartment buildings in Denver. Only the Altamaha and the Colonnade (one block west, Tour stop 17) are still standing. Both buildings were completed in 1902 in a sophisticated Renaissance Revival style, although they were the products of different architects. The Altamaha has a wide recessed central bay spanned by an arcaded stone porch topped by balconies. Flanking wings feature different window designs on each story, as well as central inset entrances and projecting balconies on the upper stories. The building is crowned with a band of evenly spaced medallions, a bracketed frieze, and a widely overhanging cornice with modillions.

Although apartment construction in Denver began in 1875, many Capitol Hill homeowners still opposed the construction of multi-family buildings in 1902. Elegantly designed luxury apartments resembling large, expensive houses made such development more acceptable. The richly elaborated Altamaha originally encompassed twenty-four units of five to seven rooms each. Innovative interior features included an internal telephone system and switchboard that connected residents with the city telephone system and an underground parking garage—an unheard of domestic amenity of the time. The *Denver Republican* described the facility as "a cellar for automobiles into which the machines may be driven by an inclined plane, and where they may be cared for by an attendant and be always at the call of the owner." The convenient streetcar access and wide range of shopping options nearby made the development even more attractive.

In the early 1980s, Kent Riddle turned the historic Altamaha Apartments into office suites.

20 HAMILTON APARTMENTS
1475 HUMBOLDT STREET

D&L

Architectural Style: MISSION REVIVAL
Built: 1908   Cost: $80,000
Architects: WILLIAM COWE AND GEORGE F. HARVEY

The popularity of the Mission Revival style during the early 20th century is illustrated by the dark red brick Hamilton Apartments erected in 1908. The style is reflected in features such as the curvilinear parapets with round vents filled with iron scrollwork, corner towers with overhanging bracketed eaves, and wrought iron balconies. The front of the three-story building faces quieter Humboldt Street and features an elaborate brick and wrought iron entrance gate with a stone plaque inscribed with the building's name that accesses the enclosed front courtyard. Mrs. M. Schwartz commissioned architects Cowe and Harvey to design the $80,000 apartment house erected by builders McGrath and Stewart.

21 COOPER HOUSE/STANLEY FURS
1600 EAST COLFAX AVENUE

Architectural Style: HOUSE WITH COMMERCIAL ADDITION
Built: CIRCA 1895   Cost: UNKNOWN   Architect: UNKNOWN

The avenue's original character is found in the stately residence erected by Kemp G. Cooper, visible behind a 1938 commercial addition. The large two-and-a-half-story house has a steeply pitched roof with shingled dormers at the corners and brick walls with stone trim. The house occupies a prominent location at Park Avenue's terminus with East Colfax Avenue. The first owner served as president and general manager of the Republican Publishing Company, which produced the *Denver Republican* newspaper. Architect George H. Williamson resided in the house while designing the 1925 East High School (see Tour stop 33). He died here in 1936 after a long illness. In 1938, a $4,000 addition was constructed on the front of the house. Stanley Furs occupied the storefront from the 1930s to the early 1980s.

The Hamilton Apartments' architects, William Cowe and George F. Harvey, also designed houses in Capitol Hill and Park Hill.

This house with commercial addition is a highly visible landmark at Park Avenue and East Colfax.

22 BOHM-GRIFFITH HOUSE/ INGLENOOK APARTMENTS/ HOLIDAY CHALET HOTEL
1820 east COLFAX AVENUE

Architectural Style: MISSION REVIVAL
Built: **1896, 1923** Cost: UNKNOWN Architect: UNKNOWN

Stately single-family residences lined East Colfax Avenue and intersecting streets during the late 19th century. Henry Bohm, a New Yorker with a jewelry business in the mining town of Leadville, moved to Denver in 1880 and established a successful and long-lived firm. While most of the state languished as a result of an economic depression beginning in 1893, Bohm's wealth was such that he built this fine two-and-a-half-story brick home with stone trim and a Tiffany stained glass window in 1896.

Noah and Ida Griffith obtained the house in 1912 as their family home. Following Noah's death during the Spanish Flu epidemic in 1918, Ida converted the building into the Inglenook Apartments in order to provide an income to raise her three children. A 1923 expansion included twin two-story porches on the east and a two-story addition at the rear, creating twelve efficiency apartments catering to widows. Amenities included Murphy beds, private bathrooms, and kitchens. In the 1950s, John and Margaret Griffith, Ida's son and daughter-in-law, converted the building into a hotel known as the Holiday Chalet, "where every day is a holiday." To prepare for the task of managing the establishment, Margaret attended classes in hotel management and executive housekeeping at the Emily Griffith Opportunity School. The interior was remodeled into units with one or two rooms and electric kitchens. Now a bed and breakfast, the Holiday Chalet draws guests from around the world.

In 1923, Henry Bohm's former home was converted into an apartment building with Mission Revival style additions and interior remodeling.

23 ACOBO BUILDING
1900 EAST COLFAX AVENUE

Architectural Style: MEDITERRANEAN REVIVAL
Built: CIRCA 1928 Cost: UNKNOWN Architect: UNKNOWN

The three-story Acobo Building is one of the finest of the 1920s buildings constructed along the avenue. Its composition of brown brick and terra cotta is crowned by a hipped parapet with brown and orange tiles. Multiple first story storefronts are clad with terra cotta, and most retain their original eight-light transom panels. Of note is the separate, set back, one-story apartment entrance with curvilinear parapet and terra cotta elaboration on the west. The building features retail and service spaces on the first story and apartments above. Original businesses in the Acobo included a ladies' clothing shop, a barber, the Yale Laundry Company, a bakery, a Hoover vacuum cleaner shop, and a meat market.

24 KRUSE RESTAURANT/PETE's KITCHEN
1962 EAST COLFAX AVENUE

Architectural Style: 20TH CENTURY COMMERCIAL/ART DECO
Built: CIRCA 1936 Cost: UNKNOWN Architect: UNKNOWN

To get your fill of the East Colfax scene, squeeze into Pete's Kitchen with the crowds craving its abundant breakfasts, cheeseburgers, and Greek specials. Pete Contos, the owner, came to the U.S. from Greece in 1955 and created an eight-restaurant empire. Contos is said to have introduced gyros to the city and has been instrumental in the development of "Greek Town," a section of the avenue east of Colorado Boulevard. In the 1980s, he began his ownership of this small one-story red and buff brick corner building with the angled corner entrance. Ralph E. Kruse's mid-1930s restaurant was the first business in this building. By 1939, Mrs. Geneva E. Laxon's Restaurant served food from this location. Bill's Kitchen Restaurant (later "The Kitchen") began at this address in the 1940s.

Terra cotta is employed on the cornice, slightly projecting bays with curvilinear parapets and cartouche ornaments, and the spiral-columned quoins.

The neon sign at Pete's Kitchen is considered a classic, as is that of the Satire Lounge to the west.

25 THE LEETONIA
2021–2033 EAST COLFAX AVENUE/1515 VINE STREET

Architectural Style: ART DECO
Built: 1930 Cost: $70,000
Architect: WALTER H. SIMON

The elegant Leetonia, an Art Deco style apartment house with commercial spaces facing the avenue, was built during the Great Depression by Sitler and Company, a real estate firm headed by Charles W. Sitler. The $70,000 building replaced a large historic residence on the site. The street level on the south encompassed seven storefronts. Early businesses included an auto tire shop, a restaurant, a meat market, a dry goods concern, a clothes cleaning business, and a beauty parlor. Tailor Nathan Smernoff fashioned suits in the building for more than two decades. The Aladdin Beauty Shop, which derived its name from the popular movie palace at East Colfax and Race Street, styled the hair of neighborhood residents during the period after World War II.

The Leetonia is one of the finest examples of Art Deco style architecture in the city. The building's large mass is divided into bays by parapets and slight projections, and the surface of the brick walls is enlivened by spandrels of decorative brickwork between the abundant windows of the upper stories. Exquisite terra cotta with stylized plant and geometric forms ornament the tops of the parapets, the lintels of the second story windows, and the highly elaborated apartment entrance on Vine Street. The first story storefronts also feature a terra cotta cornice, cladding, and fluted columns with Art Deco capitals.

The architect, Walter H. Simon, graduated from the University of Illinois and moved to Denver in the early 1920s. He worked as a draftsman in the offices of architects Fisher and Fisher before establishing his own firm in 1925. One of his first important projects was the design of the PenCol Apartments at 504 East Colfax Avenue (see Tour stop 10) in that year.

The Vine Street entrance to the second story apartments presents a fine display of Art Deco style terra cotta.

The Leetonia Building at 2021–2033 E. Colfax is ornamented with decorative brickwork and polychromatic terra cotta.

26 WEICKER TRANSFER AND STORAGE COMPANY
2100 EAST COLFAX AVENUE

Architectural Style: ITALIAN GOTHIC
Built: 1925 Cost: UNKNOWN
Architects: WILLIAM E. AND ARTHUR A. FISHER

The fortress-like appearance of this eight-story building provides a clue to its function. The Weicker Transfer and Storage Company erected this storage depository for household goods and specialty items in 1925. During that era, many people were moving from single-family houses into apartments and dividing larger dwellings into multifamily buildings, resulting in the need for a storage structure. Some neighbors mounted an unsuccessful legal challenge to the building's construction, arguing that such a facility would attract rats and encourage juvenile delinquency. By contrast, a local publication at the time praised the Weicker property as "an example of an industrial building so pleasing architecturally that it adds rather than detracts from the residential district in which it stands." The building offered 70,000 square feet of storage space, a freight elevator, two large safes, and special rooms to hold furs, Oriental rugs, and works of art.

Robert V. Weicker established the moving firm in 1888. He had previously worked for wholesale druggist W. A. Hover. With Hover's encouragement and a $300 loan, Weicker began a delivery and moving service using horses and wagons. The company grew, motorized, and joined thirty other moving firms in creating Allied Van Lines in 1928. This building continues to be used for storage of personal items.

The noted architectural firm of brothers William E. and Arthur A. Fisher designed the building, reportedly drawing inspiration from city halls in Florence and Siena, Italy. The Italian Gothic style is reflected in features such as the rooftop crenellation, Gothic arch arcade, travertine marble walls, wrought iron balconets, triangular window pediments, hanging wrought iron lanterns, and the projecting face of the wall near the top of the building. This is the tallest building, and one of the most distinctive, along the avenue.

The eight-story Italian Gothic design for Weicker Transfer and Storage Company features walls clad with travertine marble.

27 SAVAGEAU BUILDING/ WALGREEN'S DRUGSTORE
2226–2260 EAST COLFAX AVENUE

Architectural Style: MEDITERRANEAN REVIVAL
Built: 1930 Cost: UNKNOWN
Architect: HARRY W. J. EDBROOKE

Canadian Jacob Savageau came to Denver in 1874 as the sales representative for the Armour Beef Company. In 1880, he founded the Solitaire Coffee and Spice Company and Jacob Savageau and Co., merchandise brokers. Solitaire ground and roasted coffee beans as well as nuts for peanut butter and designed the famous Brown Palace coffee blend. Jacob Savageau retired from business in 1917, but became interested in real estate and development, resulting in the construction of this building in 1930. He hired architect Harry Edbrooke, who produced a beautiful Mediterranean Revival design.

Walgreen's drugstore occupied the east end of the building from the time it opened until the mid-1950s. Charles R. Walgreen founded the chain in Chicago in 1901 by acquiring an existing pharmacy and transforming it with brighter lighting, wider aisles, a more diverse product line, and improved personal service. He also expanded the soda fountain menu to include sandwiches, soups, pies, and cakes. By 1929 there were 525 Walgreen's stores across the country. After World War II, the company revolutionized the retail drug trade by introducing self-service shopping in its stores.

In 1974, the Rainbow Grocery opened in the former Walgreen's location. The Divine Light Mission of Guru Maharaj Ji, a teenage boy who came from India to lead a yoga commune on York Street, owned the store. Carrying organic produce and natural food products, the Rainbow Grocery served as a Denver pioneer in the health food market. Wild Oats acquired the business in 1989, and it continued to offer groceries at this location through the late 1990s. Other businesses that operated in the building included a Piggly Wiggly grocery, florist Edwin Schu, a Gamble's auto supply and home improvement store, liquor stores, and Savageau Gallery, owned by Jacob Savageau's grandson.

This highly decorative example of the Mediterranean style is notable for its polychromatic ornament and projecting corner tower.

28 CAPITOL HILL STATE BANK
2239 EAST COLFAX AVENUE/1509–1515 YORK STREET

Architectural Style: CLASSICAL REVIVAL
Built: 1925 Cost: $100,000
Architect: JOHN M. GARDNER

When the Capitol Hill State Bank completed this building in 1925, this section of East Colfax Avenue was the fastest developing part of the thoroughfare. Denver architect John M. Gardner, who also designed several buildings for the Gates Rubber Company in south Denver, produced drawings for the imposing $100,000 brick and terra cotta building. The bank occupied the first story, while the upper stories contained offices leased by other businesses. A safety deposit vault with a capacity of 2,000 boxes was one of the special interior features. Terra cotta resembling stone lavishly embellishes the front wall, which features a frieze inscribed with the name of the bank and two-story fluted pilasters. The Capitol Hill police station was conveniently located on the east side of the building at 1515 York Street until 1932.

When the bank was finished in August 1925, merchants along East Colfax Avenue between Race and Elizabeth streets held a carnival celebration and open house featuring the businesses of the street. The bank kept its doors open to allow visitors to examine the new facilities. The *Denver Post* commented, "It probably is the first case on record of a crowd waiting in line just to look at the interior of a bank." The financial enterprise closed by the end of the year after one of its vice presidents was convicted of embezzlement.

The second floor of the building housed the offices of a variety of businesses over the years, including insurance, oil, and architecture firms, lawyers, advertising agencies, and an organization known as "The Get Acquainted Club." The third floor provided space for doctors' and dentists' offices until the 1950s. Mrs. Olive H. Cochran's beauty parlor replaced the police station around the corner, staying there from the mid-1930s into the 1970s.

THE FRONT OF THE 1925 CAPITOL HILL STATE BANK IS DOMINATED BY TWO-STORY FLUTED COLUMNS.

29 PARK VIEW HOTEL/YORK VIEW APARTMENTS/MIERLEY CLINIC/ GOLDEN APARTMENTS
2301 EAST COLFAX AVENUE/1510 YORK STREET

Architectural Style: RENAISSANCE REVIVAL
Built: 1914   Cost: UNKNOWN   Architect: UNKNOWN

In 1914, the Colfax Investment Company built this substantial three-story hotel, one of the few large buildings so far east on the avenue at that time. Known as the Park View, it included forty rooms on the upper stories and commercial spaces on the first floor. The elegant brick building features a widely projecting cornice, a variety of arched windows with ornamental crowns, and balconies above an elaborated entrance on the west wall.

During the 1918–1919 Spanish Flu epidemic, *Rocky Mountain News* reporter Katherine Anne Porter lived here. She incorporated her experiences at the time into a novel entitled *Pale Horse, Pale Rider*. By 1924, the building had become the York View Apartments and included nine residential units. Two years later, Dr. Ira C. Mierley acquired the property and converted the upper stories into a private medical clinic and hospital. Mierley, who attended Jefferson Medical College, moved to Denver for his health in 1902. Two years after his hospital opened, one of Dr. Mierley's patients charged him with lunacy, and the State Medical Board investigated and revoked his medical license. After his death in 1930, Mierley's wife, Ida, lived here and established the nine-unit Golden Apartments on the upper stories. Businesses on the first story included the York Hardware Company, the York Drug Company, and Barrymoore's Restaurant.

John Weems Hand, Jr., described as "the model of the counter-culture businessman," acquired the building about 1980 and operated his antique store and investment firm here. In 1989, this building became the headquarters of Hand's Colorado Free University, which is still offering a diverse range of adult, continuing education, and nontraditional educational courses from this location.

THE PARK VIEW HOTEL
FEATURED FORTY ROOMS
WITH SHARED BATHS
ABOVE THE COMMERCIAL SPACES
OF THE FIRST STORY.

30 AUSTIN BUILDING
2400–2418 EAST COLFAX AVENUE / 1472 JOSEPHINE STREET

NR DL

Architectural Style: RENAISSANCE REVIVAL
Built: 1904; 1908, 1910, 1918 (ADDITIONS) Cost: UNKNOWN
Architect: AUDLEY W. REYNOLDS

Denver native Frank A. Austin purchased a prominent corner site and erected this three-story buff magnesium brick building to house luxury apartments, including his own and one for his parents. The building also contained his drugstore on the street level at the northwest corner. The Austin Building was completed in four stages: the original central component in 1904; an apartment addition to the south in 1908; and one-story retail expansions on the east in 1910 and 1918.

The building faced one of the city's major streetcar-serviced avenues, ensuring high visibility for its commercial spaces and convenience for its apartment residents. Austin's Pharmacy, founded in 1895, operated one block further west on the avenue until moving into this building in 1904. The Strickland Pharmacy, a chain, occupied the corner space from 1921 to 1934, followed by the Capitol Drug Company. Frank Austin worked as a pharmacist for Capitol Drug until it closed and he retired in 1950. Austin lived here until his death in 1966, and his wife resided in the building until 1970. The other storefronts attracted a variety of businesses, including a florist, interior decorating company, plumbing and heating firm, furniture repair shop, delicatessen, furniture store, and clothes cleaner.

Denver architect Audley W. Reynolds, who maintained a residence here for six years, designed the building as a restrained expression of the Italian Renaissance Revival style with differing window treatments on each story, Ionic columns, brick quoins, an enriched cornice, and a horizontal emphasis provided by rock-faced sandstone courses. The building contained eleven apartments, each with five to seven rooms incorporating the latest technologies. Quality materials were utilized throughout the interior. Five light wells brought sunshine and ventilation to the apartments, which featured mountain views. No other examples of Reynold's work are known to exist in Colorado.

The Austin Building features an angled northwest corner, name and date of construction plaques, and a western porch and balconies.

31 BLACK AND WHITE AUTOMOTIVE SERVICE/MAACO
2424 EAST COLFAX AVENUE
Architectural Style: MODERNE
Built: 1949 Cost: $32,000 Architect: UNKNOWN

A filling station was demolished to make way for this building, an addition to the Black and White Taxi Company garage to the south. David S. Day operated the Black and White Automotive Service here from 1950 into the early 1980s. East Colfax Avenue attracted many automobile service companies, including gas stations, garages, parts houses, and dealerships. The two-story, L-shaped building is a very good example of the Moderne style, with a steel frame and a curtain wall of glazed tile blocks, rounded northeast and northwest corners featuring stacked square blocks, rounded metal coping, and a projecting metal-trimmed canopy with a curved corner on the east.

32 FIFTH CHURCH OF CHRIST, SCIENTIST D☒L
1477 COLUMBINE STREET
Architectural Style: ITALIAN RENAISSANCE
Built: 1921, 1929 Cost: $215,000
Architect: HARRY W. J. EDBROOKE

The first services in the Fifth Church of Christ, Scientist took place on Thanksgiving Day 1929. Organized in 1919, the congregation worshipped in the Bluebird Theater before erecting this building. In 1920, the church bought lots at the corner of East Colfax and Columbine and engaged Harry W. J. Edbrooke to design its new place of worship. The church was constructed in two stages — the basement level, offices, and reading rooms in 1921 and the superstructure in 1929. The massive Italian Renaissance style building displays a red tiled hipped roof, a wide classical entablature, terra cotta-trimmed tan brick walls, and a granite foundation. Three two-story arches with paneled entrances, bracketed terra cotta panels, and arched windows dominate the north and east façades.

A POPULAR CHOICE FOR 1930s-1940s TRANSPORTATION-RELATED BUILDINGS, THE MODERNE STYLE EVOKED A SENSE OF STREAMLINED SPEED.

THE CHURCH'S TWO-STORY HIGH AUDITORIUM COULD SEAT MORE THAN FIVE HUNDRED PEOPLE COMFORTABLY AND FEATURED A REUTER PIPE ORGAN.

33 EAST HIGH SCHOOL AND CITY PARK ESPLANADE
1545 DETROIT STREET

NR DL

Architectural Style: JACOBEAN
Built: 1925   Cost: $1,470,000
Architect: GEORGE H. WILLIAMSON

Denver Public Schools built beautiful East High School to address increasing student enrollment and to provide a modern replacement for its 1889 predecessor in downtown Denver. The four-story mottled red brick building with light gray terra cotta trim and seven-story clock tower has often been compared to Independence Hall in Philadelphia. Gray Ozark marble and statuary in the building's lobby, a state-of-the art auditorium, and a grand double staircase represented Denver's commitment to providing students with an inspiring learning environment. Large windows ensuring ample natural light and ventilation to classrooms were a requirement of the school district. The exquisite library on the third floor was restored in 2006. The library features a Hugh Walter mural depicting Marco Polo's travels that was added during the 1930s as a Works Progress Administration project.

East became a model for other high schools and was considered an architectural ornament for the surrounding community. The architect, George H. Williamson, a Colorado native and 1893 graduate of East High, won an architectural competition for the design commission. Williamson also worked on Teller Elementary School and Smiley Junior High School in Denver. He lived a short distance west of East High in the 1920s and 1930s (see Tour stop 21).

Reflecting the school district's City Beautiful policy of locating schools adjacent to parks on sites with commanding vistas, East High, with its own eleven-acre campus, faces the City Park Esplanade, a two-block long formal entry to the park from East Colfax Avenue dating to the 1900s. The 1917 Sullivan Gateway includes figural sculptures of miners and pioneer women designed by Leo Lentelli of New York to represent agriculture and mining. The associated Dolphin Fountain rises from a shell-shaped basin.

From East Colfax Avenue the Sullivan Gateway leads to East High School and City Park.

34. BONFILS MEMORIAL THEATER/ HENRY LOWENSTEIN THEATER
2526 EAST COLFAX AVENUE/1475 ELIZABETH STREET

Architectural Style: MODERNE
Built: 1953 Cost: $1,250,000
Architect: JOHN K. MONROE

The Bonfils Memorial Theater served as Denver's major entertainment venue when it opened in 1953. Denver-born John K. Monroe designed the blond brick building in a Moderne style he described as combining "dignity and simplicity of appearance." Theater patron and philanthropist Helen Bonfils provided funding in memory of her parents, Belle and Frederick G. Bonfils. The opening night celebration attracted hundreds who admired the interior's elegant travertine and wood paneling. The dedication program for the Bonfils in 1953 asserted, "No community theater in America—and few, if any, professional theaters—has a more beautiful home than this nor one as carefully planned and equipped for the purpose." The Denver Civic Theater, founded in 1929 in association with the University of Denver, utilized the facility for more than thirty years, with Helen Bonfils providing creative direction for its high quality productions. The multipurpose theater also accommodated operas, movies, concerts, lectures, and television.

Construction of the Denver Center for the Performing Arts in the 1970s drew the spotlight away from the Bonfils, which focused on community theater. In 1985, the theater was renamed in honor of Henry Lowenstein, a Jewish immigrant from Germany who attended Yale and produced a number of shows here during a thirty-year period. The 37,000-square-foot building closed in 1986 and sat empty and in increasing disrepair. The *Perry Mason* television series, filmed in Denver in the early 1990s, utilized the facility. In May 2005, St. Charles Town Company acquired the theater and adjacent land, initiating an award-winning $16 million retail development that preserved the historic building. The Tattered Cover Bookstore and Twist & Shout Records, two highly successful homegrown businesses, anchor the complex, which includes a new parking structure, the Denver Folklore Center, restaurants, and other stores.

Denver's famous Tattered Cover Bookstore occupies the former Bonfils Theater.

35 THE DETROIT
2801 EAST COLFAX AVENUE

Architectural Style: LATE 19TH AND EARLY 20TH CENTURY REVIVALS
Built: 1904   Cost: $35,000   Architect: T. ROBERT WIEGER

Charles Fisher financed this apartment building at East Colfax and Detroit Street in 1904. A branch streetcar line to City Park ran north on Detroit Street, possibly influencing the decision to build at what was then some distance from downtown. The Detroit marks the farthest eastward extent of large apartment buildings built along East Colfax Avenue by the early 1900s. Frank Kirchoff, one of Denver's most prominent contractors during the first half of the 20th century, built the apartments. T. Robert Wieger, Kirchoff's in-house architect, designed the building. The Detroit provided apartment residences for several decades and was reborn in the early 1950s as the O'Riley Building, which contained several life insurance agencies, a realtor, a dental lab, and a dentist.

36 LOUSTANO HOUSE/ VOGEL PLUMBING AND HEATING
3000–3002 EAST COLFAX AVENUE

Architectural Style: HOUSE WITH COMMERCIAL ADDITION
Built: PRE-1904, 1946 (ADDITION)   Architect: UNKNOWN

Many large residences built along and adjacent to East Colfax later became rooming houses and apartment buildings. Some gained commercial additions, providing space for small businesses. The original two-story Foursquare brick house with Classical Revival style details dates to before 1904 and has a 1946 one-story commercial component facing the avenue. Notable architectural features of the original house that are still visible include the pedimented dormer with Palladian motif window, ornamental terra cotta plaque, decorative glass, and bay window. Silvin Riche Loustano, a Colorado native and successful Denver dentist, was an early owner. Conrad H. Vogel built the one-story 1946 addition for his plumbing and heating company.

The Detroit's substantial size and original architectural details provide indications of its importance in 1904.

Construction of commercial additions attached to large houses was a popular trend along the avenue after World War II.

37 MEYER's KOSHER MEATS
3201–3217 East COLFAX AVENUE

Architectural Style: 20th Century Commercial
Built: 1922, 1923, 1926   Cost: $14,000   Architect: unknown

These three buildings are examples of "taxpayer blocks"—inexpensive rental buildings that defrayed investors' costs until increasing land values justified constructing more substantial structures. Tenants in this seven-storefront building have included Meyer's Kosher Meats, Elbert Cheese and Dairy Store, and Collins Bicycles.

38 HAGANS JEWELRY/BLOCK FLORAL
3220–3242 East COLFAX AVENUE

Architectural Style: Early 20th Century Commercial
Built: 1930, 1934   Cost: unknown   Architect: unknown

This dark brown brick multiple-storefront building displays lavish applications of blue, yellow, and cream terra cotta. Diverse small businesses operated by longtime tenants included the jewelery store of Orville R. Hagans; Melville L. Block's florist shop; Russian immigrant Joseph Bitman's clothes cleaners; and New Yorker Harry M. Papazian's Oriental rug and carpet store.

39 INTEMANN CANDIES/ GOODSTEIN'S DELICATESSEN
3221–3237 East COLFAX AVENUE

Architectural Style: 20th Century Commercial
Built: 1922   Cost: $6,000   Architect: unknown

Grocer and theater operator John Thompson erected this six-storefront building. The buff brick walls have dark brown brick trim. Notable occupants have included Harry Intemann Candies and Goodstein's Delicatessen, operated by Harry J. Goodstein, grandfather of Denver historian Phil Goodstein.

THESE 1920s AND 1930s ONE-STORY CORNER COMMERCIAL BUILDINGS HOUSED A VARIETY OF NEIGHBORHOOD-ORIENTED RETAIL AND SERVICE BUSINESSES OVER THE YEARS.

40 THOMPSON THEATER / BLUEBIRD THEATER
3315–3317 EAST COLFAX AVENUE

Architectural Style: ECLECTIC
Built: 1914 Cost: UNKNOWN
Architect: HARRY W. J. EDBROOKE

This 1914 theater was the first in Denver designed solely for the screening of movies. Originally named the Thompson Theater after its owner, grocer John Thompson, it featured second-run films that had already played downtown. Harry W. J. Edbrooke designed the building soon after establishing his own architectural practice. In addition to planning significant buildings in downtown Denver, Edbrooke completed several along East Colfax. The success of this theater led Thompson and his partner-manager J. A. Goodridge to erect the Ogden Theater in 1917 (see Tour stop 14, also by Edbrooke). In 1921, Harry Huffman purchased the Thompson as part of the city's first and largest locally owned chain of movie palaces and renamed it the Bluebird. Huffman has been called "the most powerful single voice in the development of popular entertainment and culture in Denver in the first half of the 20th century."

Like other theaters in Denver during the 1930s, the Bluebird attracted patrons by offering raffles and drawings for free prizes. Bank nights, when a lucky theatergoer won cash, were among the most popular events in the Huffman chain, and continued for 613 weeks at the Bluebird. During the 1940s, the Bluebird sold more war bonds than any other in the Huffman group. The theater's decline began after the war, due to the changing nature of the avenue and deferred building maintenance. After a brief stint presenting art films, the theater began showing adult movies in 1974 and attracted the attention of anti-porn protesters. During this period, much of the façade was covered with nonhistoric materials. The screen went dark in 1987 after seventy-three years of projecting motion pictures. A $500,000 rehabilitation in 1994 restored much of the exterior and created a venue for live performances in the auditorium.

THE THEATER'S PROJECTING PIE-SHAPED MARQUEE DATES TO THE 1930S.

JOHN THOMPSON'S 1914 BLUEBIRD THEATER LATER BECAME PART OF HARRY HUFFMAN'S CHAIN.

41 BASTIEN's RESTAURANT
3503 EAST COLFAX AVENUE

Architectural Style: MODERN/GOOGIE
Built: 1958 Cost: UNKNOWN Architect: WILLIAM B. BASTIEN, SR.

William B. Bastien, Sr., former manager of a dime store who came to the United States from his native Alsace-Lorraine, purchased the existing Moon Drive-In at this location in 1937. Under his ownership, waitresses on roller skates delivered American fare to customers and the original drive-in underwent a number of expansions. Bastien's empire eventually included five other restaurants in the Denver area.

In 1958, Bastien tore down the old building and erected this eye-catching replacement, which may be the only twelve-sided restaurant in the Denver area. The owner reportedly developed the design. The shallow, conical, folded plate roof with a domed skylight at its apex was likely influenced by the Googie architectural movement (see Tour stop 11) of the late 1950s and early 1960s. The structure resembles a flower from the air. The imposing neon sign and unusual building shape were undoubtedly intended to impact passing motorists on U.S. 40, as well as hometown residents. The restaurant is surrounded with ample paved parking.

Bastien continued to operate the restaurant until his death in 1969. It is still owned and run by his family members. In 2006, historian Tom Noel observed that "Bastien's is still a time capsule to cherish," noting that it offers "the best, most affordable steaks in town."

The Bastien family has operated their restaurant in this building for nearly fifty years.

42. NATIONAL JEWISH HOSPITAL
3800 EAST COLFAX AVENUE

Architectural Style: VARIOUS
Built: VARIOUS Cost: VARIOUS
Architects: WILLIAM E. AND ARTHUR A. FISHER;
T. ROBERT WIEGER, AND OTHERS

People seeking the health benefits of Denver's fresh air and sunshine began arriving almost as soon as the city was founded. The climate seemed to be particularly restorative for those suffering from respiratory diseases, especially tuberculosis. Also known as consumption, the condition brought thousands to Denver in search of a cure. The Jewish Hospital Association formed to provide medical care for those who could not afford it and obtained this site. The Frances Wisebart Jacobs Hospital, honoring Denver's "Queen of Charity," was completed in 1893, but a national economic crisis prevented it from opening.

In 1899, the Jewish organization B'nai B'rith provided financial support and the hospital began operating. Since most funds came from outside the state, it was renamed National Jewish Hospital for Consumptives. The nonsectarian institution dedicated itself to "humanity, to our suffering fellow man, regardless of creed." Tuberculosis treatment often involved lengthy stays, so National Jewish instituted patient educational and social programs, including English instruction.

Now known as National Jewish Medical and Research Center, this institution is the only one in the nation focused exclusively on the research and treatment of lung, allergic, and immune diseases. The campus includes thirteen buildings and encompasses approximately twenty acres. The architecture ranges from the 1922 Colonial Revival style Beaumont Nurses' Home with its fine east-facing portico designed by T. Robert Wieger, to the 93,600-square-foot Iris and Michael Smith Clinics and Laboratories dedicated in 2007. Of particular interest is the 1927 B'nai B'rith Building on the east side of Colorado Boulevard, designed in a grand Renaissance Revival style by the noted Denver architectural firm of W. E. Fisher and A. A. Fisher. Finely crafted terra cotta elaborates the three-story central entrance arch. Above the doors is the original hospital motto: "None may enter who can pay, none can pay who enter."

The newest building at the hospital, the Iris and Michael Smith Clinics and Laboratories, was dedicated in May 2007.

Images of a ram and bull are included in the beautiful terra cotta surrounding the B'nai B'rith Building's entrance.

Photo: Roy Hyskell photograph, 1926, Denver Public Library, Western History/Genealogy Department,

43 DENVER ORPHANS' HOME/ DENVER CHILDREN'S HOME
1501 ALBION STREET

Architectural Style: RENAISSANCE REVIVAL
Built: 1902 Cost: $34,538
Architects: WILLIS A. MAREAN AND ALBERT J. NORTON

Since its opening in 1902, this building has served Denver's children. The institution's history began with the Denver Ladies' Relief Society. Organized in 1873, the Society's goals were to establish a home for the homeless and destitute and to provide temporary assistance to those suffering from sickness, accidents, and other misfortunes. The group quickly came to believe that the care of children should be separate from that of the elderly and infirm. In 1880, several prominent Denver women incorporated the Denver Orphans' Home Association with the goal of creating a residence for children without parents. They completed a new facility in 1883.

The Home shifted its mission to providing temporary shelter and care for "needy, neglected, and dependent" children in 1898, after the state began serving orphans. Children from six months through twelve years were admitted, including those from homes with divorced parents, ill parents, working mothers, and no mothers. By 1900, 125 children were living at the institution.

The Home acquired this site and raised funds from subscribers throughout the city to complete the building in 1902. Willis A. Marean and Albert J. Norton drew the plans, and a contemporary account described the building as "the most complete, roomy, sunny, happy place of all the public institutions." Beginning in 1921, the top floor operated as a hospital. Albion, a public elementary school across the street, exclusively educated the Home's children after 1923. The residents also participated in a variety of educational, recreational, and social activities designed to prepare them for their return to normal family life. The institution's name changed to Denver Children's Home in 1962, and it began providing residential therapy and counseling for children with emotional problems, becoming the first Colorado facility to offer such treatment outside a hospital setting.

This C-shaped building has
many large windows providing
abundant sunlight to the interior,
as shown in this 1920s view.
Photo: Authors' Collection

44 WEISS DRUG STORE
5001–19 EAST COLFAX AVENUE

Architectural Style: MODERNE
Built: 1928, 1946 (CORNER ENTRANCE) Cost: $16,000
Architect: UNKNOWN

Contractor Marvin Riggs erected this multiple storefront building in 1928 for David Lavine. The long one-story building originally contained seven storefronts. A drug store occupied the building's west corner from its construction through the early 1980s. George P. Fry operated the drugstore in the late 1920s and early 1930s, followed by Lustig Drug in the mid-1930s. The Weiss Drug Company dispensed prescriptions for more than forty years. Proprietor Fred Weiss gave the angled corner entrance its distinctive appearance. A $7,500 remodeling by the Grant R. Watson Construction Company resulted in a rounded corner, a new parapet wall, and variegated green terra cotta tiles. The source for the tiles installed in 1946 is not known, although the Denver Terra Cotta Company was still operating at that time.

45 EASTMOOR BEAUTY SHOP
5724–5736 EAST COLFAX AVENUE

Architectural Style: 20TH CENTURY COMMERCIAL
Built: 1946 COST: $40,000 Architect: UNKNOWN

This four-storefront building represents modern architectural influences that impacted the one-story strip shopping structures built along the avenue after World War II. Helen Ginsburg financed construction of the building erected by N. R. Neilson and Son in 1946. The flat roof building is composed of concrete block walls faced with variegated red and brown brick. The front displays narrow bands of buff brick and cream terra cotta coping. Each storefront has an angled inset entrance with a terrazzo floor embedded with a metal street address number. The shops include plate glass display windows with transoms above and glazed black tiles below. Businesses serving the nearby residential areas of Eastmoor and Crestmoor leased the spaces.

The Elm reflects the remarkable decorative effects of architectural terra cotta.

This retail building served the Eastmoor and Crestmoor neighborhoods and housed a beauty shop, a furniture store, and clothing stores.

46 MILLER's GROCETERIA/ MILLER's SUPER MARKET
7150 EAST COLFAX AVENUE

Architectural Style: 20TH CENTURY COMMERCIAL
Built: 1946 Cost: $40,000 Architect: UNKNOWN

The Miller's Groceteria chain built this large one-story building to house one of its new supermarkets as part of a multi-million dollar expansion of the company in the late 1940s. Abe Perlmutter Construction erected the structure, which has concrete block walls faced with brick and arched steel roof trusses. The band of large plate glass windows facing East Colfax Avenue displays a glass block transom panel above and colorful bright blue tiles below.

Several thousand customers jammed the store when it opened in September 1946. The supermarket boasted of ten high-speed check stands, wide aisles, special refrigerator showcases, "daylight fluorescent lighting," and a lighted half-block parking lot. The *Rocky Mountain News* called it "the West's largest grocery store."

Miller's Groceteria traced its roots to 1903, when Jay Miller opened a small grocery in Denver. In 1919, Morris "Moe" Miller, Jay's son, started an expansion program. The chain became the first in Denver to integrate grocery, meat, and produce into one supermarket operation and was the first to open self-service meat departments. This concentration of services in one-stop supermarkets spelled the demise of large numbers of small individual neighborhood grocers, meat markets, bakeries, produce shops, and creameries. In 1957, National Tea Company acquired Miller's Super Markets for $7 million, retaining the name. Miller's operated forty-three stores in Colorado and Wyoming by 1966, with twenty-eight in the Denver area. The chain adopted the name Del Farm in 1969 and has since disappeared from the Denver grocery scene.

A Colorado chain of groceries, Miller's Groceteria, built this supermarket with a wide expanse of display windows facing the avenue and a large parking lot to the east.

47 CHICKEN DELIGHT
7676 EAST COLFAX AVENUE

Architectural Style: MODERN
Built: CIRCA 1953 Cost: UNKNOWN Architect: UNKNOWN

This 1953 restaurant building housed a Chicken Delight franchise. Al Tunick founded the Chicken Delight chain in Illinois in 1952. Tunick hit upon the idea of deep frying breaded chicken coated with spices. Previously, chicken was considered a poor fast-food choice because of its relatively long cooking time. With Tunick's method, the chicken cooked quickly but remained juicy. The concept was franchised, and the chain soon expanded to more than 1,000 locations. The restaurant's slogan, "Don't Cook Tonight—Call Chicken Delight," was aimed at mothers and working women. Chicken Delight remained at this location until the late 1950s. The number of Chicken Delight outlets declined in the mid-1960s. The company is now headquartered in Canada.

The Howard House restaurant offered meals here from the 1960s through 1970, followed by the Jolly Coffee Shop until 1983. The western-themed Ranch House Café, the present tenant, occupied the building in about 1985.

Chicken Delight did not provide a standard design for its franchises. This corner location shows off the building's distinctive roof shape. Two asymmetrical intersecting gables rise from the center outward, sheltering the walls below. The roof plane dips downward at the northwest corner and massive beams are exposed on the gable ends. Creating a remarkable appearance with a striking modern roof design was one way to establish a distinctive identity and attract customers. As a writer in *Pencil Points* (later *Progressive Architecture*) remarked in 1943, "the time is not far distant when . . . walls and roofs will follow the sweep of the sun and the stars."

THIS BUILDING WITH SOARING ROOF PLANES HOUSED A CHICKEN DELIGHT RESTAURANT.

48 WESTERNER MOTEL
8405 EAST COLFAX AVENUE

Architectural Style: MEDITERRANEAN REVIVAL
Built: 1949 Cost: $32,000 Architect: UNKNOWN

As part of U.S. 40, a major transcontinental highway, East Colfax provided a logical location for travel-related businesses. Several postwar motels concentrated in the eastern part of the thoroughfare sport signs with western or Native American themes. Contractor George Erickson built the Westerner Motel for Harry T. Reese in 1949. The U-shaped motel's office is located at the south end of the west wing. The facility captures a southwestern theme with its red tile roof and white stucco walls.

49 SAND AND SAGE MOTOR COURT
8415 EAST COLFAX AVENUE

Architectural Style: MEDITERRANEAN REVIVAL
Built: 1946 Cost: UNKNOWN Architect: UNKNOWN

The Sand and Sage Motor Court, not pictured, is a U-shaped motel with a tall bell tower with arched openings near the northeast corner and a detached office located in the central court. Mediterranean influences include the red clay tiles, stucco walls, and gabled parapets defining entrances.

50 LAZY-C MOTOR LODGE
8787 EAST COLFAX AVENUE

Architectural Style: RANCH
Built: 1950 Cost: UNKNOWN Architect: UNKNOWN

The Lazy-C Motor Lodge is an L-shaped motel with a one-story northern leg and a two-story western wing with office and attached porte-cochere. The walls are composed of oversized bricks with extruded mortar joints. Contractor Joe Martin constructed the motel for the Collins Investment Company.

THE DISTINCTIVE SIGNS ASSOCIATED WITH MOTELS ALONG THE AVENUE WERE IMPORTANT ADVERTISING FEATURES.

SELECTED SOURCES

Coel, Margaret. *The Colorado State Capitol*. Denver: Colorado General Assembly, 1992.

Colorado Historical Society. Office of Archaeology and Historic Preservation. Historic site survey forms and National and State Register nomination forms. Denver, Colorado.

Denver Public Library. Western History and Genealogy Department. Photographs and Clipping files. Denver, Colorado.

Goodstein, Phil. *Denver's Streets*. Denver: New Social Publications, 1994.

_____. *Ghosts of Denver: Capitol Hill*. Denver: New Social Publications, 1996.

Hess, Alan. *Googie: Fifties Coffee Shop Architecture*. San Francisco, California: Chronicle Books, 1985.

Langdon, Phillip. *Orange Roofs, Golden Arches: The Architecture of American Chain Restaurants*. New York: Alfred A. Knopf, 1986.

Longstreth, Richard. *The Buildings of Main Street: A Guide to American Commercial Architecture*. Washington: The Preservation Press, 1987.

Massey, James C. and Shirley Maxwell. "Houses of Homes: The Origins of Apartments." *Old House Journal* 22 (November–December 1994).

Merry, Paul R. "An Inquiry into the Nature and Function of a String Retail Development: A Case Study of East Colfax Avenue, Denver, Colorado." Doctoral dissertation. Northwestern University, Evanston, Illinois, 1955.

Noel, Thomas J. *Denver Landmarks and Historic Districts*. Niwot, Colorado: University Press of Colorado, 1996.

Noel, Thomas J. and Barbara S. Norgren. *Denver: The City Beautiful and Its Architects, 1893–1941*. Denver, Colorado: Historic Denver, 1987.

Simmons, R. Laurie and Thomas H. Simmons. "Capitol Hill Neighborhood." Denver Neighborhood History Project. Prepared for the City and County of Denver, Denver Landmark Preservation Commission and Office of Planning and Community Development. Denver: Front Range Research Associates, Inc., January 1995.

Smiley, Jerome C. *History of Denver.* Denver: Times-Sun Publishing Co., 1901; reprinted Denver: Old Americana Publishing Co., 1978.

Stewart, George R. *U.S. 40: Cross Section of the United States.* Boston: Houghton Mifflin Company, 1953.

Whitacre, Roger. Personal Interview, Denver, Colorado. By R. Laurie Simmons and Thomas H. Simmons. 23 February 2007.

Witzel, Michael K. *The American Motel.* Osceola, Wisconsin: MBI Publishing Company, 2000.

Wyckoff, William. "Denver's Aging Commercial Strip." *Geographical Review* 82 (July 1992):282–94.

Selected Index

Armet and Davis, 32
Aronoff, Henry, 30
Austin, Frank A., 66

Bastien, William B., Sr., 80
Bettcher, George L., 48
Bohm, Henry, 52
Bonfils, Helen, 72
Bowman, William N., 16
Brown, Alexander, 28
Brown, Henry C., 14
Buell, Temple H., 16

Capitol Hill State Bank, 62, 63
Cedar Investment Co., 20
Clements, William F., 32

Cohen, Samuel, 34
Colfax Investment Company, 64
Collins Investment Company, 92
Contos, Pete, 54
Cooper, Kemp G., 50
Coquard, Leon, 26
Cowe, William, 50

Denver Public Schools, 70

Edbrooke, Frank E., 14, 38
Edbrooke, Harry W. J., 38, 60, 68, 78
Erickson, George, 92
Ervin, Raymond Harry, 22
Fallis, Montana, 18
Fifth Church of Christ, Scientist, 68

Fisher, Charles, 74
Fisher, William E. and Arthur A., 56, 58, 82
Flower, John S., 42

Gardner, John M., 62
Garrison, Robert, 16
Ginsburg, Helen, 86
Goodridge, J. A., 38, 78
Gove, Aaron M., 26
Griffith, John and Margaret, 52
Griffith, Noah and Ida, 52
Gumry, Peter, 14

Harvey, George F., 50
Holmberg, John, 44, 48

Jackson Realty & Investment Company, 24

King, Otis Archie, 22
Kirchoff, Frank, 74

Lentelli, Leo, 70

Mammoth Skating Rink Co., 34
Marean, Willis A., 84
Martin, Joe, 92
McMann, Robert H., 20
Mierley, Dr. Ira C., 64
Miller's Groceteria, 88, 89
Miller's Super Market, 88
Monroe, John K., 72
Moorman, Edwin H., 34, 42
Morris, Milton, 30
Muchow, William C., 22
Murdoch, James, 14
Musick, George Meredith, Sr., 16
Myers, Elijah E., 14

National Jewish Hospital for Consumptives, 82

National Jewish Medical and Research Center, 82
Neilson and Son, 86
Norton, Albert J., 84

O'Brien, Arthur H., 20

Quayle, Charles, 44

Reese, Harry T., 92
Reynolds, Audley W., 66
Rice, Eugene R., 28
Richey, Luzerne A., 28
Riggs, Marvin, 86

Savageau, Jacob, 60
Schrepferman, Conrad, 28
Schwartz, Mrs. M., 50
Seckler, Warren C., 46
Seerie and Varnum, 16
Silver State Savings and Loan Association, 22
Simon, Walter H., 28, 30, 56
Sitler and Company, 56
Sitler, Charles W., 56
Snyder, George, Jr., 18
St. Charles Town Company, 72

Thompson, John, 38, 76, 78

Vogel, Conrad H., 74

Walsh, Thomas F., 26
Walter, Hugh, 70
Watson Construction Company (Grant R.), 86
Weicker Transfer and Storage Company, 58, 59
Weiss Drug Company, 86
Wieger, T. Robert, 18, 74, 82
Williamson, George H., 50, 70
Willison, Robert, 18